Andalusian "The Noblest Horse in the World"

Horse Books For Kids

Nature Books for Kids

By

K. Bennett

JD-Biz Publishing

Read More Amazing Animal Books

Purchase at Amazon.com

Andalusian

Table of Contents

Introduction

He knows when you're happy
He knows when you're comfortable
He knows when you're confident
And he always knows when you have carrots.
~Author Unknown
***

Andalusian: The Andalusian horse is a very special horse that comes from the Iberian Peninsula. They are strong, well-built and very elegant. They also have a beautiful mane and tail, which is long and thick.

The ancestors of this "***Pure Spanish horse,***" have lived on the Peninsula for thousands of years. Can you remember what a Peninsula is? In our book "*Colonial Spanish for Kids*" we talked a little about this.

What is a Peninsula?

The dictionary describes a Peninsula as: '*A piece of land almost surrounded by water or "coming" out of a body of water*.' The Iberian Peninsula is located at the southwest part of the European continent. If you would like to see it on a map, ask your parent or a guardian to help you search.

What makes Andalusians so special?

For many thousands of years, Andalusian horses were known as excellent war horses. But Royals or nobles also loved these beautiful animals, and used them to help the government make deals with other countries.

Andalusians are family to another type of horse called the **Lusitano** of Portugal. Long ago, both of these horses were thought to be the same type, but after the 1960s that changed. Now the Lusitano is one type of horse and the Andalusian is another type.

As mentioned before, these horses are elegant, which means they know how to look good! But they also have a beautiful personality. They are known as docile (Calm and kind), and sensitive.

Andalusians: past and present

In the beginning, Andalusians were used for many different activities like: Dressage, bullfighting and as a stock horse. Have things changed over the years? What do you think?

Today, Andalusians are still used in dressage, but now their activities include show jumping and driving. Oh, and did I tell you they can act too? Can you remember watching an Andalusian in a movie? It might have been a historical or fantasy film. No? Then later on, I will tell you which movies they were in. You might know some of them!

A horse by any other name

Did you notice Andalusians are called a "***pure Spanish horse***?" This is only one of its names. It is also called a "purebred Spanish horse" and a **PRE**. Can you guess what these letters mean? It means: **Pura Raza Española.**

Although they are known as a Spanish horse, Andalusians helped a lot of other horses around the world. Different European and American horses came from Andalusians. Horses like: Friesian, Lipizzan, Mustangs, Peruvian, Paso Fino and more!

With their beautiful personality and rich ancestry, Andalusians are wonderful horses to learn about. Please take a moment to read a little more about this noble animal, and don't forget to share what you learn with others!

WOULD YOU LIKE TO DRAW A SIMPLE HORSE? LEARN HERE!

Wikihow.com has a simple, but neat tutorial on drawing horses. Here are the steps to get started:

1- **First,** ask your parent's or a guardian's permission to go online.

2- In your browser (Chrome, Internet explorer, Firefox, Torch) type: www.Wikihow.com

3- In the search box at the top of the page type: *Draw a simple horse.* Once the search is complete, you should see a title that reads: "**How to draw a simple horse: 11 steps with pictures**."

4 – Click on the link and follow the steps.

5- Have fun!

Andalusian

Chapter 1

Hi, just out for a stroll!

History: To understand Andalusian history, we have to go back in time to the courage of Gladiators, famous coliseum games and leaders called Emperors. Have you guessed where this is? Yes! It's the Roman Empire.

In those days, Andalusian horses were adored by everyone. They were also loved and their owners thought they were precious! Do you have anything you really, really love and that's very important to you? That's how people felt about Andalusian horses!

The Roman circuses were full of these beautiful animals and spectators loved watching them perform!

We can even go further back than the Romans to 20,000 BC (Before Christ). Cave paintings showed beautiful pictures of Andalusian ancestors on the walls. Traders like Phonecians and Celts helped the horse to get to other places too. How did they do that?

When the traders traveled from place to place, they brought the horses from other parts of the world with them. Many traders came from places like Northern Africa to trade. And when they traded the horses, their horses mixed with other horses and soon Andalusians were on the way!

During the middle ages, Andalusian horses were known far and wide, thanks to famous men like Abd al-Rahman III. And in the XVI century Don Diego Lopez gathered mares and studs to create the well-known Royal Stables of Cordoba.

And in the year 1667, a man by the name of William Cavendish (Duke of Newcastle) called the Andalusian horse a "prince" of horses. He also said they were very intelligent! Of course they were not like the horses we know today, but they were close! And they worked very hard with the Royal family not only at their homes or castles, but also in riding academies.

Andalusians were also used as stock horses to work with dangerous bulls! And even today, many of these beautiful horses are used in bull fighting events. They also participate in many types of horse shows and show jumping! (Source: *Wikipedia.org*)

DO YOU REMEMBER?

Do you remember the different types of horses and what it means? For example: What is a mare? What about a stud? Let me list them so you will have a better idea of what it means!

Horses, like us, have different titles for different stages of life. For example when a horse is born until 6 months of age it is called a *foal*.

Then up to the age of 2 years it is called a *yearling*. If the horse is a male horse it is called a *colt* under the age of 4. When it is older than 4 years it is called a *stallion*. Do you remember what a Stallion is?

Meaning of Terms:

A *stallion* is a: Male horse that can have kids.

A *gelding* is a: Male horse that cannot have kids. (Geldings are usually patient, calm, quiet and well behaved.)

A young female horse or pony is called *filly* and after the age of 4, she is called a *mare*. (Source: *Lessonpaths.com*)

A stud

The word is an Old English word that means: "herd of horses, place where horses are kept for breeding." (Source: *Wikipedia.org*)

So a stud is a horse used to have baby horses. And of course people only want the best daddy horses to have the best baby horses!

This is so much fun!

This is a neat way to measure horses. The measurement refers to hands, literal hands! The symbol is usually HH (Hands high). So you would say 15hh, 16hh or 17hh. This means 15 hands, 16 hands and 17 hands. You might be wondering why people measure horses in hands?

Well, many years ago people did not have rulers or measuring sticks like we do today. So they used whatever they had…and they had hands. So horses are measured like this. You can do it too! How?

Think about it like this: One hand is 4 inches.

So if a horse is 15 hands multiply this by 4. (15 x 4) and you will get 60 inches. And if a horse is 16 hands multiply this number by 4. (16 x 4) and you will get 64 inches.

Now that you know how to do it, you can measure other horses for yourself. Have fun!

Andalusian

My hooves are getting cold!

Strengths: Andalusians are great horses with an elegant **gait**. Do you remember what a gait is? It simply means the way the horse walks! This makes them very good at dressage competitions. Do you remember what dressage is? In our "*Cleveland Bays for Kids*" book, we wrote about this skill, but I will repeat it again for you!

Dressage training: Dressage training has been around for a very long time. The USDF (United States Dressage Federation) organization lists different levels for this type of skill.

There are five levels:

-Training level
-First level
-Second level
-Third level
-Fourth level

Andalusian

Before you begin this type of training, there are several things to do. *Wikihow.com* suggests the following steps.

1- Both you and your horse need to know each other very well! And you need to know if you can trust each other. So a close relationship is very important before any training can begin!

2- You have to start to work on the way your horse walks or trots. This is referred to as a **gait**. It is very important for your horse to walk in the right way.

3- **Transitions:** This is when you want your horse to change from one movement to another. It is important to do this smoothly. It should be just like putting one footstep in front of the other without tripping over your feet!

4- Your position in the saddle should look comfortable and balanced! And your heels should be down at all times.

5 – Practice makes perfect. To get good at any skill, you need to do it over and over again. Practicing with your horse is a great way to get good at riding him!

Of course there are many other steps to dressage that is very important. But these are some of the basic ideas. If you want to learn more, ask your parent or a guardian to help you research!

Andalusians are also great *Show Jumping*. Do you know what type of sport this is?

Show Jumping: You may already know that show jumping has to do with… jumping! But how does it work?

Well, the horse has to navigate or make its way across different types of obstacles or barriers. This happens inside a stadium or ring designed for these types of shows. During these events the horse is tested in different ways. For example, your horse will be tested for:

-Strength
-Stamina
-Speed and
-Flexibility…

And these skills are all very important. But wait…there's more! The horse also has to show its relationship with the rider. In other words, horse and rider should ride as one! So if you participated in this type of event, you and your horse should have a very, very good relationship. And more importantly, you need to be close friends!

Why is this important? Guess who loses points if your horse makes a mistake? Yes! Both of you lose points, not just your horse. And if your horse decides not to make enough jumps, both of you will be disqualified. Ouch! Do you see why being friends with your horse is so important?

Weaknesses: With such an amazing horse, do you think they have weaknesses? Sadly, yes! We all get to a point where we can't do some activity or thing we would like to do, right? The same happens to Andalusians. They get a sickness called ***Laminitis*** if they eat too much. Have you ever heard of the name before? If you haven't, ask your parent or a guardian to help you research what this means.

Their skin color is also lighter than other horse breeds, which leaves them more exposed to the strong rays of the sun. This means skin problems like ***melanomas***. Again, if you do not know what this means, look it up in the dictionary or ask a parent or guardian to help you!

(Source: ***Horses.animal-world.com***)

Out for a walk with mommy!

Characteristics: Andalusians have lots of different names. You have already learned about a couple of them. Would you like to hear more? They can be called:

-The Iberian saddle horse
-The Iberian war horse
-Extremeno
-Zapata
-Villanos
-Castillian
-Alter Real
-Spanish horse and more!

Height: Approximately 15 to 15 ½ hands.

Weight: 900-1200 pounds. Some may weigh a little more or less, but this is the usual weight.

Coats: Andalusians have beautiful standard coat colors like gray or bay. But did you know most of the horses are just these two colors? There are also other exotic colors like chestnut, palomino, black and dun, but these are not easy to find.

Will you be my friend?

Chapter 2

Walking around town

Have you learned anything new about Andalusians? Wonderful! But there is still a little bit more we can learn about them. How about training? We will detail the steps for training all horses and then give you additional tips on training Andalusians! Ready?

Training: *Wikihow* recommends the following steps to train horses:

1-*First of all, don't scare the horse*. That means you should not run up or sneak up on them and go boo!! This is not a hard to understand. Do you like it when people run or sneak up on you suddenly? It may scare you when someone does that, right? Then a horse will feel the same way.

2-*Be gentle and talk gently to your horse*. There is no need to yell, shout or talk in a harsh tone to your horse. Again, this idea is not hard to understand. Do you like it when people talk to you gently? Or do you want them to shout and yell at you all the time? Isn't it nicer to treat others kindly, and don't you like it when others do the same for you? Your horse will appreciate your kind manner too!

3-*Most horses love to be touched*. Show them your feelings through your hands. Stroke them on the head, massage their neck, hug them, brush them and communicate your affection through gentle fingers. Imagine how happy your horse will be!

4-*Try to spend as much time as you can with your horse*. In any friendship, regular visits are the key! No matter what you have to do, stop by and visit your horse just to remind them that you're there. They will be so happy to see you and the more you spend time with them, the stronger your bond will grow.

5- *A nice reward*. A tasty treat, rub or pat down, yummy food, grooming of whatever other treat you might have in mind, will be a great idea! Do this at the end of the day to let your horse know how much you enjoyed spending time with them.

Andalusian training skills: Andalusians are easy keeper horses! This only means they are easy to care for. So if you wanted to get one, this might be a great choice. You won't have to give them tons and tons of food and they won't get too fat!

Their mane and tail is very beautiful and very thick, so you will have to brush them a lot. They also need a trim from time to time.

Training them is not as hard as other horses, because they are kind and eager to make you happy. But don't forget to treat them with respect. If you don't, you might have big problems to train them!

GENERAL HORSE TIPS FOR KIDS:

If you have a horse or if you plan to get one in the future, you will need to care for it. So here are some other tips you can think about: (Source: Frank Bell- *Horsewhisperer.com*)

-Your horse's diet is very important. Some horses have very hot blood and some have cooler blood. If your horse has hot blood, they will need less protein in their diet.

-Learn how to properly discipline your horse. Remember: These animals are very sensitive and in the case of Andalusians, they are very intelligent. Let them know when they are getting too out of control! This can be with a shhhhh noise or a firm tone to let them know who is in control.

-If the horse's head is high it means your horse is not relaxed. They may be uptight. If their head is low they are relaxed. Try to ensure your horse is always relaxed. This will help them feel good and both of you will enjoy the ride.

-Horses love to get your tender rubs and soft patting. Things like rubbing their ears, nose, eyes and mouth is great. A gentle massage is even better!

Andalusian

Remember:

-If a horse is trained really well, he or she will invite YOU for a ride. You should be looking for the invitation! Then you know you will enjoy an awesome ride.

-Your horse can sense your moods and behavior. If you are confident your horse will be confident too!

-You should feed your horse from a bucket and not your hand. (This is the recommendation, but I feel it is better to feed them with your hand from time to time! It seems to generate more trust and respect, but that is just my humble opinion on the subject. What do you think?)

Chapter 3

The wind feels good!

Training a horse is a great, but knowing what horses are like is also great. This will help you to understand what is going on behind their bright, curious eyes! Think about this:

-A horse can express its emotions in many different ways. It can use its face, eyes and ears to tell you how it feels!

-Horses are great at keeping watch. It is rare to see a herd with everyone snoozing at one time. There is usually one horse standing as a lookout, and his job is to warn the others if danger comes near!

- Avoid standing behind a horse. They have great vision, but there are a couple of blind spots. Can you guess what the back part of the horse is? Yes! It's a blind spot. If the horse gets angry or scared, guess what he might do if you stand directly behind him?

Andalusian

-Horses are great at listening! They can turn their ears in different ways to improve their hearing. If you whisper and say something bad about your horse, they just might hear you!

- Horses can help people get better when they have mental or health problems. This is called: ***Equine Assisted Therapy***.

-Horses are the best sleepers on the planet. They can sleep lying down and standing up! Can you do that?

- Horses are herbivores. Do you know that this means? It means they eat plants or are plant eaters, if you like this term better.

-Horses have feelings and emotions too! Treat them kindly with lots of patience and love. You may be surprised at the results! (Source: ***Onekind.org***)

I can see you!

Andalusian

INTERESTING FACT FOR KIDS:

Andalusians are great actors and actresses! Here is a small list of movies to give you an idea!

-Gladiator
-The Cradle of Life
-Braveheart
-Lara Croft, Tomb raider
-The Lord of the Rings trilogy and more!

And during the 2002 World Equestrian games, Andalusians took home two bronze medals! Can you guess for which discipline? ***Dressage!*** The same team that won the bronze medal came back in 2004 for the summer Olympics, and this time, they won the silver medal!

Way to go Andalusians!

Andalusian

Conclusion:

Thanks for reading about me!

In conclusion: Horses are beautiful creatures, and Andalusians are no different! This strong, sweet and intelligent horse is a wonderful example of amazing Earth creatures.

And this is a great time to learn a bit more about them. You may be surprised at what you find out. If you don't know where to look, ask your teacher, a parent or guardian to help you. They may have some great ideas too!

If you don't know exactly what to research about this horse type, then think about this: Why don't you choose something you really like (It can be the tail, mane, ears, body, size, personality, history, etc) and learn a bit more about that particular subject? For example: Are they warm blooded or cold blooded?

In the case of Andalusians, you could research how they are so important to European culture. How did it make a difference in Europe? What is the difference and why is it important? But wait, here's another idea…

You could research what makes Andalusians so great at dealing with bulls. What do they do when a bull is angry or just in a bad mood? And when the bull charges, how does the Andalusian get out of the way so fast…without getting hurt?

What is "*regal carriage*?" What does it really mean? If you do not know what it is, look it up!! Or ask your parent or guardian to explain it to you.

Another option is this: If you are in school and you participate in show and tell, use that as your subject. Many of your classmates may not even know what an Andalusian is really like, so it would be nice to share what you find with others!

I hope this book has taught you just a little how wonderful nature is, and how much fun it can be to learn about each of its creatures! Don't forget that what we learn today, can affect our lives tomorrow!

And remember: *"Educating the mind without educating the heart is no education at all."* - *Aristotle*

Author Bio

K. Bennett loves to write for both children and adults. Many different subjects are interesting to develop, but writing for children is special to her heart.

Her favorite pastimes include reading, traveling and discovering new things. Each of these activities helps to fuel her imagination and acts like a blank canvas waiting for more stories.

She is intrigued with fantasy elements like hidden worlds and faraway lands. Basically anything that gets her imagination soaring to new heights!

Her writing credits include children books online, short stories for online magazines, and two novellas listed at Amazon.com

Our books are available at

1. Amazon.com

2. Barnes and Noble

3. Itunes

4. Kobo

5. Smashwords

6. Google Play Books

Publisher

JD-Biz Corp

P O Box 374

Mendon, Utah 84325

http://www.jd-biz.com/

Mendon Cottage Books

P O Box 374, Mendon Utah 84325

Andalusian

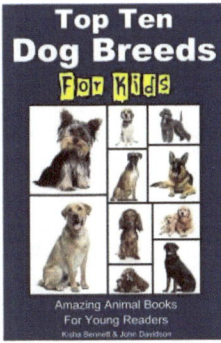

Top Ten Dog Breeds For Kids

Amazing Animal Books For Young Readers

Kisha Bennett & John Davidson

German Shepherds

Dog Books for Kids
K. Bennett

Bulldogs

Dog Books for Kids
K. Bennett

Dachshund

Dog Books for Kids
K. Bennett

Poodles

Dog Books for Kids
K. Bennett

Labrador Retrievers

Dog Books for Kids
K. Bennett

Rottweilers

Dog Books for Kids
K. Bennett

Boxers

Dog Books for Kids
K. Bennett

Golden Retrievers

Dog Books for Kids
K. Bennett

Puppies

Dog Books For Kids

Amazing Animal Books
By John Davidson

Beagles

Dog Books for Kids
K. Bennett

Yorkshire Terriers

Dog Books for Kids
K. Bennett

Dogs
Top Ten Dog Breeds For Kids

Amazing Animal Books
For Young Readers
Zahra Jazeel & John Davidson

Cats For Kids

Amazing Animal Books
For Young Readers
K. Bennett & John Davidson

Foxes For Kids

Amazing Animal Books
For Young Readers
Zahra Jazeel & John Davidson

Wolves For Kids

Amazing Animal Books
For Young Readers
By John Davidson and Virginia Fidler

Andalusian

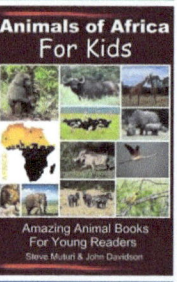

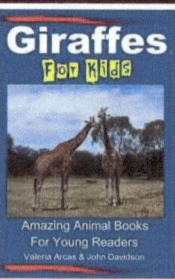

Andalusian

Andalusian

www.ingramcontent.com/pod-product-compliance
Lightning Source LLC
Chambersburg PA
CBHW050911290526
45792CB00002B/774